All rights reserved, no part of this publication may be either reproduced or transmitted by any means whatsoever without the prior permission of the publisher

VENEFICIA PUBLICATIONS UK
veneficiapublications.com
veneficiapublications@gmail.com
Typesetting © Veneficia Publications UK
October 2020
Text ©Diane Narraway.
All images are from the public domain.

A bit of 'this n that' from the poetic cauldron of Diane Narraway

QUITE FUNNY

A MIDSUMMER NIGHTMARE
THE TRUTH ABOUT FAERIES
NEIGHBOURHOOD WITCH
THE FERRYMAN
THREEFOLD RULE
THE WITCHES WARNING!!
WITCHFINDER GENERAL & THE WITCH
FLYING OINTMENT
URBAN OCCULTIST
ROMEO AND JULIET (SORT OF)

A BIT SEXY

I WANT
DAEMON LOVER
LUST
TRUE LOVE
VAMPYRE
CONTROL
THE ETERNAL KISS
FOLLOW ME
VISITOR OF THE NIGHT
DEATH'S SWEET KISS
JUST ONE BITE
BLOOD AND FIRE
WHAT IS IT YOU WANT?

SLIGHTLY PROFOUND

LUCIFER'S LIGHT
OCEAN MAGICK
MOONCHILD
COMMUNION
PHASES OF THE WITCH
CONNECTED
INSIGNIFICANCE OF MAN
ANCIENT ALTAR STONE
THE BEAT OF MY HEART
THE FOOL AND THE MAGE
FORGOTTEN CHILDREN
PLANETARY INVOCATION
FIRE DRAGON
LESSON ONE
LOVE BEYOND RELIGION
LET THERE BE LIGHT
DREAMSTATE
ANOTHER LIFE
POWER OF THE WITCH
TODAY
SOUL SENSES
SONG OF THE PHOENIX
THE WITCH
SWEET UNCERTAINTY

Diane Narraway

QUITE
FUNNY
A BIT
SEXY
&
SLIGHTLY
PROFOUND

INTRODUCTION

They say that you can learn a lot about someone through their poetry. In this instance all I can say is 'Gods I hope not!'

That said, I guess there has to be a bit of me in here somewhere, albeit a strange and slightly dark bit.

There will be some who read this who have seen some of my "Quite Funny" selection performed by me, and a few others crazy enough to get up, dress up and join me. I hope they bring good memories and a smile or two. Of course, should any of you fancy putting on a half hour pantomime, please feel free to use any of the poems in here – they are as much fun to perform as they are to watch.

I considered including a dedication but then decided against it. I figured that if you think any of my poems are about you, whether funny, sexy, or profound - well who knows? Maybe they are.

Most of all, I hope all those who read this book enjoy it - it is, after all, quite funny, a bit sexy and slightly profound!

Diane Narraway

QUITE
FUNNY

A MIDSUMMER NIGHTMARE

(HELLEQUIN)
From Harlequin, to Hellequin
I make the change this night,
While faeries work their magic,
And pixie turns to sprite.

In mischief beyonfd compare,
Most worthy of a cheer,
Oberon shall marry Titania
In the wedding of the year.

And without further ado,
Bring the couple hither now.
So, we who are gathered
Can witness their wedding vows.

Oberon do you take this woman
To be your lawful wedded wife?

(BOTTOM)
It'll be the first woman
He's ever taken in his life!

(PUCK)
And by woman he means,
Common or garden tart.
Ask any of the pirates
That drink in the white hart.

(HELLEQUIN)
And do you take this man
To love honour and obey?

(BOTTOM)
What! Obey slack Oberon?
There's no effing way!

(HELLEQUIN)
And should you be poor or rich
Healthy or inflicted by the pox.
I fear she may have the latter
Based on her love of cocks!

And will you love each other
According to the natural law?

(BOTTOM)
Just how is this natural?
He's a queen n she's a whore!

(HELLEQUIN)
Now comes the time for you both
To make your sacred vows.

(PUCK)
Oberon ... don't you promise anything
To that dodgy old cow!

(OBERON)
My body and all that I have
With this ring, I do thee wed.
Granted my body's not up to much
But I'm a superstar in bed!

(TITANIA)
And I too offer you my ring,
To say that I'm all yours,
In every conceivable way,
You can even have me on all fours!

(HELLEQUIN)
And now we reach the time
When Oberon must kiss his bride,
And I pronounce them very loosely,
To be man and wife.

And let me introduce the Lady Bottom,
Titanias partner in crime.

(BOTTOM)
We share the booze, we share the men,
But here's where I draw the line.

(HELLEQUIN)
And also, Oberons best man
The one, the only, inimitable Puck.

(PUCK)
Get your minds out of the sewer,
We've already pushed our luck.

Besides, I'm filled with envy.
In fact, I'm positively green,
For I had always hoped
I'd be Oberon's faerie queen.

(HELLEQUIN)
But we must not forget Oberon,
Nor Titania his new wife.
Who come tomorrow morning,
Will get the shock of their life.

For when the spell is broken
In the mornings early light,
They face that eternal question,
'What the hell did we do last night?'

Oh, I do so love mischief,
And forsooth the mirth;
Midsummer surely must be
The greatest night on Earth

And will Oberon have to pay
When he awakens from his sleep
Titania's going rate? ... Trust me,
Her services aren't cheap.

But for now, without further ado,
We celebrate with ale and hearty fayre
As we welcome every one of you,
To this midsummer nightmare.

THE TRUTH ABOUT FAERIES

They seem so small and dainty
Such delicate little things,
As pretty as a picture,
With fragile cobweb wings.

But where angels fear to tread
Faeries rush straight in.
More deadly than an Exocet,
Is that cheeky faerie grin.

It's true, they really do wear boots,
And their aura packs a punch.
Frighteningly mischevious
They're completely out to lunch.

And though they're natures guardians,
And they *really do* grant wishes.
The twinkle in a faerie's eye,
Can't half be bloody vicious.

But if you're blessed enough
To call one a friend or wife,
Then the twinkly eyes and faerie smile
Will be the best thing in your life.

NEIGHBOURHOOD WITCH

Dear councillor Johnson,
I wish to complain,
About those two witches
From next door again.
I called my dog in
Just the other night,
When I was confronted
By a terrible sight.
Stood over a cauldron,
Wearing pointy black hats,
Chanting and dancing
With their familiar black cats,
And quite honestly councillor
All this bell book and candle,
Is rather too much
For us decent folk to handle.
Our nice quiet estate
Has gone to the dogs,
And we now live in fear
Of being turned into frogs.
And they may eat our children,
Or seduce our men,
And tell me councillor Johnson
What will happen then?
Please don't think I'm prejudiced

Or out to cause grief,
But if you could house them elsewhere,
It would be a relief.

Dear Mrs Longbottom,
I understand your concern
But it's quite clear to me,
You have a lot to learn.
Your families are safe;
These women aren't bad,
And your lack of knowledge
Is really quite sad.
Its another belief,
I can't condemn them for that.
Nor can I rehouse them
For owning a cat!
And would you be writing a letter
If they were Hindu or Jewish,
Muslim or Mormon,
Catholic or Amish?
So, let me reiterate.
Your kids will not
End up in the oven.
I know this for sure,
As I'm part of their coven!

THE FERRYMAN

Working on the premise,
Things are never as they seem,
I kept all my fingers crossed
That this was just a dream,
Because a cold dark riverbank,
Had replaced my cosy bed,
And now it would appear
There's a damn good chance I'm dead.

And it didn't take me long
To realise I was not alone,
Or that we were all about to reap
Exactly what we'd sown,
And judging by the crowd
It had been a busy night,
Which was of little consolation
As the ferry came in sight.

And when it finally reached the shore
A shout came from the crowd,
'Just who the bloody hell are you?"
But the ferryman just bowed,
Tipped his hat, winked his eye,
And with a flash of his gold crown,
Said in a market traders voice,

"Now let's see who's fer goin' up
'N' who's fer goin' dahn!"

Armed menacingly with a clipboard,
And a little stubby pen
He smiled menacingly
As he scanned the list
Of those who'd been condemned.
"Now when I call out your name,"
His smile broadened to a grin,
"You can rest assured
You'll be paying for your sin.

Firstly! Perverts and fornicators,
Especially you ...Your Grace,
'Cos for members of the clergy,
We can always find a space.
For there are few worse crimes,
Than, those who claim to teach
Others how/to walk in truth ...
Yet don't practice what they preach!

Next up ... those who've taken human life
Without just cause or reason.
'Cos the slaughter of the innocent
Is a universal treason,
And one man's terrorist ...
Is not another's freedom fighter,

Dress it up how you like
Your sentence won't be lighter.

As for those who took the bottle
Or the needle as their wife,
Hell won't seem too far removed
From that which you called life.
But you should be aware,"
He said with a smirk
"The drugs they sell down here
REALLY just don't work.

Now as for liars, thieves, and petty crooks
Who broke the law for kicks.
We have made some room for you,
Across the river Styx.
Although every now and then 'tis said,
He turns a blinded eye,
To the petty misdemeanors
Of those just trying to get by.

Ah! Jehovas witnesses, you're on my list
For, all that door to dooring.
And the Mormons just because
The book of Mormon is so boring.
And as for the rest of you,
Don't think you are exempt.

There's more of you going down,
You're an easy race to tempt."

My knees weren't just knocking,
They were bangin'
Like a bishop in a brothel!
Cos, I felt sure he'd call my name,
And I'd be bound for hell.
And whether I was dreaming,
Or if in fact had died,
Didn't seem to matter much
Stood on that river side.

And though relief swept over me
When he put down his list.
I still blurted out,
"Excuse me, sir,
I think I have been missed.
'Cos I'm sure in all honesty
If you look again,
Under 'Sinners Miscellaneous'
I'm sure you'll find my name."

Tell me foolish little child,
Do you suppose I cannot read?
Just what do you think you're guilty of?
Explain your evil deed.

'Cos no one ever gets past me
Not since the dawn of time,
And luckily for you right now,
Stupid questions aren't a crime!
Consider yourself lucky,
Your name is nowhere to be seen.
You must have been forgiven
And your slate has been wiped clean.

However, those whose names I've called,
Make sure you have your fare.
For if you cannot pay,
You'll be swimming over there.
'Cos there are no free rides,
As I'm sure you have been told.
And American Express will not do nicely!
We only deal in gold!!

However, those still standing on the shore,
Who are bound for Paradise
Have already paid in full,
By simply being nice.
For none of you can truly say
You could not tell wrong from right,
Or honestly believed 'free will'
Meant do what the fuck you like!

So, if by chance you should wake,
To find this was all a dream,
It would be to your advantage
To remember all you've seen.

And always be real careful
Of the path you choose,
'Cos trust me when I say to you,
This ain't no pleasure cruise.
So, buckle up real tight,
And hang on to your hats now ladies
'Cos this here ferry's turbo charged
'N my next stop is Hades!!"

THREEFOLD RULE

Thrice I'll stir the cauldron,
At the setting of the sun,
To bid you all good cheer at Yule.
Staying mindful of the threefold rule,
I ask only that my will be done
Remembering the words
"Harm ye none!"

And incantations of hope I chant,
As between the worlds I dance.
Banishing demon, ghost and ghoul,
Ever mindful of the threefold rule,
As I ask that my will be done.
Remembering the words,
"Harm ye none!"

Yet curse I most surely will,
Should anybody wish me ill.
And your nights will seem longer than your days,
For the threefold rule works both ways.
And my will shall be done ...A lot!!
So, remember these words and,
Just make sure
You harm me NOT!!

THE WITCHES WARNING!!

If you play with witches,
Be prepared to get burned,
For it may well turn out to be,
The harshest lesson you will learn.
Think twice before you set out,
To harm a witch through spite,
For they were born long ago,
In the shadows of the night.

As only a fool would imitate,
A witch's natural arrogance,
Cos witches have spent many lives,
As masters of their craft.
And if you still wanna 'Talk the talk',
Make sure you can deliver,
Lest in the middle of the night,
You wake up ...
Sweat, shake and shiver!

So, if I were you, I'd listen
And take heed of this warning,
Cos it can be a very long night,
Assuming, you reach the morning!

WITCHFINDER GENERAL & THE WITCH

(WITCHFINDER)
I am the Witchfinder General,
And generally, I find witches,
'Cos I can tell when they're nearby
By the stirring in my breeches.
Of course, the jobs made easier,
When I see that pointy hat,
And hear the familiar mew
Of Lucifer's black cat.

I must take you to my chamber,
The torture one of course,
Where you won't get a wink of sleep
'Cos I'm hung like a horse.
I mean until you have repented,
And confessed your mortal sin
Of turning from the Lord our God,
And swapping Christ for Merlin.

(WITCH)
Oh, Sir you are mistaken,
And your accusations made in haste,
For I am just an innocent girl,
God-fearing pure and chaste.

And this ain't no old witch's hat,
It just protects me from the rain,
And my cat is just a tabby,
I suggest you look again.

(WITCHFINDER)
Hmm my inklings never lie
I know you practice the black arts.
So, I will have to search your body
For any satanic marks.
For I know you are a witch,
I have watched you with your clan,
Dancing naked at your sabbats,
Well, in my head I have.

And you have all the tools of magick
Round buttocks and large breasts,
I feel my inklings are stirring ...
But there are further tests
That I really have to do,
To make absolutely sure,
That when you cast your spells
Its demonic lovers that you lure.

(WITCH)
It would appear that I lure
Weasely, shifty, little men!

And perhaps it isn't me
Who should be looking to repent.
And I only use a besom
For sweeping up the floor,
And if you think my breasts are big,
Then checkout hers next door!

(WITCHFINDER)
You know I have a little prick ...
Test I can perform on you,
To see if you will bleed red blood
Like God fearing people do.
Then I will watch you writhe in pain,
Twist, turn and undulate,
It's a dirty job you know
But someone's gotta do it!

And if that doesn't work
Then a ducking you will go,
Where you will be stripped naked
And bobbed up n down - real slow.
Until I have come ...
To decide your fate.
Then you will be tied up and burned,
Upon a well positioned stake.

(WITCH)
Not this time Witch finder.
This time you take your final bow,
So, listen very carefully
'Cos you're my little puppy now.
And this promises to be,
A nasty lesson you will learn,
'Cos in about half an hour
You'll be begging to be burned.
And from here for all eternity
I'll bind you to me as my bitch.
So, tell me know Witchfinder General
Are you still glad you found a Witch?!

FLYING OINTMENT

The fat of an unbaptised baby boy.
Juice of Smallage,
Cinquefoil, and Bane of Wolfe.
The chaste and purest Belladonna
And Henbane fit for all.

Mix treasured Jimson Weed,
With Henbane black as night,
And Mandrake uprooted by the beasts.
With just a pinch of precious Hemlock,
For those, seeking to take flight.

Add just a dash of Fly Agaric,
And the poppy in full bloom.
Stir it slow, then use it quick
Applying generously to thy broom.

For this Sabbat unguent; magic salve
There are no valid substitutes,
Favoured by the witch.
But take care with that baby fat,
Everyone knows it can burn and itch!!

URBAN OCCULTIST

I did steal old Solomons key,
And danced across his chequered floor,
Bypassing the abyss,
As I headed for the door.

Raced on through
The tunnels of set,
Cos its cold and damp
In the halls of the dead.

I swung my way Tarzan style,
Through the tree of life,
And rode the lightning flash,
Straight towards Kether's light.

And now I loiter leather clad,
Amid the astral mists,
Where I go by the given name
Of the Urban occultist.

ROMEO AND JULIET (SORT OF)

(HELLEQUIN)
The wheel of the year turns once again,
Bringing us back to this point in time.
Where we find mischief and merriment
Music, magic, dancing ... and of course rhyme.

For tis midsummer once again
And as the master of romance.
I shall find a young couple
That I can lead a merry dance.

If you recall this time last year
We saw a wedding to end them all,
When Titania married Oberon
Down at the old town hall.

But I hear the marriage itself
Was only very brief,
And I'm sure, to Puck at least,
Their divorce came as a relief.

As Oberon is once again
The only queen in the woods,

And Titania is flat on her back
In Pirate neighbourhoods.

Now, let me set the scene,
for this year's lonely hearts to meet
Upon the streets of old Verona,
A fine midsummer's treat!

This year I feel our lovers,
Are perfect for each other
Once you get past his bloodthirsty father,
And her over-protective mother.

Let us first meet Romeo
As he learns the family trade.
Unfortunately for both his ship and crew
Not too successfully I'm afraid!

(ROMEO'S FATHER)
Tortuga! Tortuga! ...Is this Tortuga??
I think it is not!!
Look Chart stars! Stars chart!
It's easy enough to plot!

Ye Gods you've been a pirate
All your bloody life,
I think we need to find you
An incredibly rich wife!

(ROMEO)
But father I just want a girl,
Who will love me just for me,
One whose love will always be true
And perhaps, write poetry.

(ROMEO'S father)
Pah poetry! We're in Verona
Reckon when we get ashore,
You should seek out Titania
She'll show you what it's for!

I hear she's partial
To a bit of Pirate here n there,
'N' let's face it a bit is all she'll get ...

(ROMEO)
Oi, that's not very fair.

Besides I don't want
Some well used old tart.
I want a woman
Who will surely win my heart.

(HELLEQUIN)
Oh, I know just the girl for him.
One who beauty knows no bounds.

The fairest maid in all Verona
Although she has kind of been around.

Ah, here she comes sweet Juliet
Whose beauty is beyond compare.
A rare and precious creature
But then so is a grizzly bear.

(JULIET'S MOTHER)
Ah my beloved Juliet you are surely
The fairest maid in all the land,
It's about time you were married off
To a wealthy powerful man.

(JULIET)
I care not for wealth or power
I want love and romance,
A man who will sing songs of love
As under the moonlit skies we dance.

(JULIET'S MOTHER)
Songs of love indeed,
Ye Gods Juliet whatever next!
You'll make do with dinner and a pint of grog,
And a quick grope like all the rest.

(HELLEQUIN)
See how the spell is cast
As their eyes gaze upon each other.

(ROMEO)
Such beauty and such grace,
All I could want in a lover.

(HELLEQUIN)
Oh, by the grace of all the gods,
This is positively delicious.
Check out the look on her mother's face,
A swarm of wasps would look less vicious!

(ROMEO)
See how she leans her cheek upon her hand,
Oh, that I were a glove upon that hand,
That I might touch that cheek.

(HELLEQUIN)
Methinks he has got it bad.

(JULIET'S MOTHER)
You...just stay away from my fair daughter,
You ... you brutish Pirate lout

(JULIET)
He's not a brute to me Mother,
He's all I've dreamt about.

Oh, Pirate is just a name & what's in a name?
For that which we would call a rose by any other,
Would surely smell just as sweet.
And he is the scent of lover.

(JULIET'S MOTHER)
But all day long they rape, and pillage,
Plunder, and then drink all night
And in between they sleep with whores ...

(ROMEO'S FATHER)
Aaarhh too bloody right!!

I fail to see the problem,
Nowt wrong with the pirate life.
So, tell me are ye loaded?
If so, we'll have her as his wife.

(JULIET'S MOTHER)
Oi, that's my beautiful daughter,
Not some prized old sow or heifer.

(ROMEO'S FATHER)
Nay madam, for they would surely be,
More attractive ... and probably more pleasure!

And tis true what you say,
I have never felt the call of duty,
But Im more than happy to pillage, n plunder
Such a fine-looking booty.

Admittedly 'avin a wench aboard
Is considered to be bad luck,
But you two is barely wenches,
And I need someone to cook n f ..

Pluck ... Pluck the chickens
To feed me hungry crew ...

(JULIET'S MOTHER)
That's a bit of a shame,
I could use a damn good screw.

(JULIET)
But Romeo Romeo
Wherefore art thou going?

(ROMEO)
Theoretically the Caribbean,
But there's no way of really knowing.

Still take my hand, bad luck be damned!
Come along for the ride.

(JULIET)
I thought that was his intention,
And you wanted me as your bride.

(ROMEO)
Oh, more than life itself,
For we are star crossed lovers.

(ROMEO'S FATHER)
Put it how you like son,
I just wanna shaft her mother!

(ROMEO)
Ah, Juliet tomorrow we set sail,
When we can both be wed,
And sail away as man and wife
Into the Caribbean sunset.

(ROMEO'S FATHER)
But tonight, we celebrate
Get drunk and do outrageous things in bed.

I'll break out the whips n chains ...
Do you prefer black or red?

(HELLEQUIN)
Gods Im better than I thought,
Forget eharmony,
For matters of love and romance,
Check out 'match dot me'.

A perfect combination,
What could possibly go wrong?
Their lives look destined to be happy,
Prosperous, and long.

But what will tomorrow bring
In the cold sober light of day?
Will Romeo wed Juliet
And her mother still get laid?

But till then Good Night, Good night!
Parting is such sweet sorrow,
That I shall say good night
Till the Nightmare ends tomorrow."

A BIT
SEXY

I WANT ...

I want inappropriate texts in the morning
from those who know the rules.
I want to dance in the footsteps,
of magicians, heretics, and fools.
I want to drink with Dionysis
until the night is well worn,
and feel Bacchus' touch
in the cold light of dawn.

I want Punk Rock,
and I want Rebel Folk.
I want a leather clad pirate
to share in the joke.
I want magick and ritual,
I want drum and bass,
I want hot summer nights,
in denim and lace.

I want to burn like
the Stellar heart of the sun,
and to rise like the phoenix
whose life's just begun.
I will hide in the shadows,
the darkest moon child,
and howl like the wolf

whose hungry and wild.
I want to ride the beast
with a smile on my face,
for mine is the demon's
sinister embrace.

And when I sleep,
I want Morpheus
to bring life to my dreams,
in the arms of lovers,
who cause my spirit,
to breathlessly scream.
I want to taste the flesh of life,
and pick its sorry carcass clean.
And you will always remember me,
as both beautiful and obscene.

DAEMON LOVER

One look across a crowded room,
And the seeds of lust are sown.
You'll dream of me
all through the night,
And I'll watch your hunger,
with inner sight.
I can feel your presence,
and smell your scent,
And taste the fire,
of lust now spent.
And whether I'm alone,
or lie with another,
I burn only for
my daemon lover.

LUST

Lip biting,
Pulse racing,
Blood pumping,
Heart pounding,
Sweat dripping,
Breath taking,
Body shaking,
Soul wrenching,
Fever quenching,
Earth moving,
All consuming,
Forever wanting ...
... You.

TRUE LOVE

Deadly sweet kisses
That soothe in the night,
While my passion and fear
Hold me so tight.
And your soul softly plays
With the strings of my heart,
Until I'm lost deep within you
Feeling all that you are,
Intensely burning,
Consumed by desire.
My eternal love
An unquenchable fire.

VAMPYRE

Black roses and lace
Promise exquisite sin,
As the sweet scent of death
Stirs something within.

And while Cerberus guards
The door to my heart,
My satanic lust
Tears you apart.

As my soul drips with blood,
I watch yours burn like fire.
As you want …
Need …
Hunger for …
The kiss of the vampyre.

CONTROL

Twist me in a lucid dream,
Make me sweat,
Make me scream.
Cover me in depraved desire:
Stoke the flames,
Fan the fire.
Feel the heat of wanton lust.
Do with me
What you must.
Swear and curse
with bitter rage,
In words from
A forgotten age.
Make me writhe,
Jerk, and wrench:
I'll be your wytch,
I'll be your wench,
I'll be here till the end of time
With passion beyond
Reason and rhyme.
And all the while you dominate,
Take control,
And subjugate,
I'll be whatever you need.
Make me burn,
And make me bleed,

And all the while
you're in control,
I will yield,
And I will fold,
And Oh,
How much I'll beg and plead,
Just for you to spill your seed.
When all is done,
and you are spent,
You will weep,
And to your God repent.
And as I drain you completely dry
I can hear your Spirit cry.
Call me succubus,
call me daemon
Who comes to you,
As darkness deepens.
So, call to me within your dreams
And enjoy it while
It's me who screams.
For I am the beast
Within your heart.
That will, one day,
Tear your mortal soul apart.

THE ETERNAL KISS

Dark Graveyard wherein lies
An ancient altar made of stone.
Draped upon this night,
As shadows dance,
In full moonlight
Dressed in animal skins and bone.

I lie in wait, arched naked
For my lover to appear:
To heed the call of my heart,
Hips slightly raised,
And legs apart,
I tremble, both with lust and fear.

I sense your presence here,
And feel your demonic breath,
As your lips brush against my skin.
Feel my faint heart,
That beats within,
For it longs to conquer death.

I hunger for the power,
Hidden in the fivefold kiss.
Obscene and highly potent,
I'm the willing prey,

In this wild hunt:
In this savage, deadly tryst.

So, linger softly with each kiss
Slowly upwards to my breasts,
Growing ever more intense,
In passionate recompense.
Taking me to greater heights,
And my soul to greater depths.

Fill me with all you are,
Satisfy my growing lust.
Between my thighs,
Deep inside,
Writhing in pure delight,
With every pulsing thrust.

My body heaves with desire
For this demon of the night,
Whose love is cold,
Yet burns my soul,
In his erotic embrace,
I long to be his bride.

I'm powerless in his arms.
His touch, his breath,
They make me sigh,
Sending shivers down my spine.

My fingernails rip his skin,
As I draw closer to my death.

The last deadly kiss upon my lips
Makes my body burn like fire,
And when he is done,
My blood shall run,
In sweet surrender to the vampyre.

FOLLOW ME

Follow me, come follow me.
For I can sense your burning desire,
and feel your eyes upon ...
Follow me.

Follow me, come follow me.
Through star kissed woods,
to a moonlit world 'neath the devil's
tree ...
Follow me.

Follow me, come follow me.
Where darkness rules, the icy heart,
and death, will our secrets keep ...
Follow me.

Follow me, come follow me.
Through the ensuing, timeless years as
we walk the blood-soaked streets ...
Follow me.

Follow me, come follow me.
And taste the lingering kiss of death,
as it melts away all your fears ...
Follow me.

VISITOR OF THE NIGHT

Along the corridors of time
Your scent disturbs my sleep.
From within the astral haze
Visiting my darkest dreams.

Satiate my scarlet lust
In the shadows of the moon,
Where every single heartbeat
Whispers a very ancient truth.

For though I partake of this world,
And all its earthy delights.
Nothing stills my restless soul
Like the visitor of the night.

DEATH'S SWEET KISS

Is there any that could love you more,
down there,
All the seasons through?
Is there ever one, you could find more fair,
Laid in the grave with you?

Is death's kiss more passionate,
Than mine could ever be?
Does queen Hel offer a greater bliss
Than ever you had with me?

Is death a soft and loving sleep
That binds you in some way?
Charmed by her sweet embrace
Held, forever in the deep.

I hear you call both night and day,
From that space below the grass.
And I keep our love through sun, and
shade,
While your soul is with the queen of
death
Down there, where you are laid.

JUST ONE BITE

Just one bite of that sweet apple
That promised love and desire,
Filled my soul with deadly passion
And my heart with raging fire.

And at the gates of eventide
Where life and death are both the same,
I am waiting in the shadows
To hear you scream my name.

Will you offer me your heart?
Or shall I take it with my kiss?
And take you in the moonlight
As the eternal succubus.

BLOOD AND FIRE

I am the blood and tears
On the battlefield,
Where is mourned the loss of brothers.
And the rose-coloured mist
Of the passionate kiss,
As the heart speaks to young lovers.

I am the dragon's fire
That burns the soul,
Of the bitter and the vengeful.
And the soft white dove
That warms the heart,
Of the caring and most merciful.

But you. You are the fever,
The bittersweet deceiver,
Whose fire rages ever dark and deep.
And your name silently drips
From my trembling lips,
Forever yours to **keep**.

WHAT IS IT YOU NEED?

I watch you in the cold night,
hiding in the shadows.
The faint streetlight,
flickering upon your pale skin,
and I see the emptiness,
of the hungry soul that lies within.

But what is it that you need,
a wife, a mistress,
a priestess or a witch?
A mother, a whore,
an actress, a piper or a bitch?

All of them will seek to inspire:
some through their wisdom,
others through desire.
Each one playing their part,
calling the tune,
summoning the heart.

So, what is it that you seek?
Art, poetry, music,
religion, romance?
Magick, mystery, science
a place in life's dance?

What is it
that will feed,
the ravenous hunger
that lies, deep in your soul?

The reflection in your eyes
as the faint streetlight,
flickers on your pale skin.
I see you in the shadows,
ravenous and raw,
ever searching
but nothing satisfies.

SLIGHTLY
PROFOUND

LUCIFER'S LIGHT

I travel along a lonely road
through the fiery depths of hell,
watched by a thousand eyes
of angels who rebelled.

Their darkened icy gaze
following my every step,
within the realms of godlessness
where Pandora's secret's kept.

And where shadows no longer dance
far beyond your world and mine.
Where Lucifer's is the only light
in the eternal night that shines.

OCEAN MAGICK

I weave my spell, on a rain swept tor,
Where the sea winds howl
And the wild beasts roar.

Where the fog rolls in till the stars are hidden,
I speak with ancient words
Long since forbidden.

And the blood-stained skies at eventide,
Kiss my heart and wrap my soul
In all the tears I've cried.

While soft shadows trace a moonlit path,
That illuminate the bay,
And call me to the dance.

Here on astral wings amid shooting stars,
I weave the magick of the night,
Lost in the Scarlet dark.

MOONCHILD

Child of the moon,
Born of the sun,
Dancing through life,
She answers to none.

She flies on the wind,
Rising higher and higher,
Wielding the pen as a sword,
Eyes blazing like fire.

Her words part the dark waters,
That run silent and deep,
Her dance wakens the Earth,
That sleeps 'neath her feet,

Her children, they flourish,
Both the serpent and rose,
As the witch born deep within,
The dark astral shadows.

COMMUNION

I have walked the serpent,
To see diamonds in the sky,
And feel the stillness of its' breath,
As time goes slowly by.

And just how sweet the serpents' kiss,
That makes my soul take flight,
And offers just a tiny glimpse,
From within the astral light.

For that erotic daemon,
Lets me see through open eyes,
Beyond the constraints of this world,
Beyond the arrogance and lies.

So shadowed by the daemon,
I hear angels sing to Pan,
While I commune with aliens,
For man is God and God is man.

PHASES OF THE WITCH

Wonder at the daughter,
of the pale new moon,
who dances through her life,
and wishes on the stars
for it goes all too soon.

Adore the chaotic ways,
of the crescent youth,
whose beauty lies,
beyond skin deep
and hides their inner truth.

Worship the matriarchal fullness
of the fertile moon,
for her belly holds
the seeds of life,
and sings creations tune.

Glorious is the aged path,
of the dark moon hag
who can finally understand,
all that youth tries
so very hard,
to hold within its hand.

CONNECTED

Ethereal faces move gracefully,
Through strands of gossamer cloud,
And prisms of light flicker,
As the sun filters through,
My half-closed eyes.
Twinkling lights pirouette,
Across rippling waters,
That softly whisper,
Their timeless song,
To dusty golden sands.
Here I sense my connection,
To all there can ever be,
Yet somehow knowing,
That I stand alone,
In the eternal chaos,
Of forever.

THE INSIGNIFICANCE OF MAN

Emerald seas and weathered cliffs
Surround the insignificance of man,
Whose dominion over this world
Is only ever slight of hand.

Yet hidden in the shadows
Of timeless black horizons,
Are the subtle hues of ancient days
From long forgotten aeons.

Where Lucifers light dances
Over waters still and deep,
As the spirit of mankind
Is woken from its sleep.

And the daughters of Pan
Revel in earthly delight,
As the fire of Prometheus
Burns forever bright.

THE ANCIENT ALTAR STONE

Let me paint a picture,
Of an ancient altar stone,
And a long-forgotten shaman
Dressed in hide and bone.

Whose piercing eyes see everything,
Behind his painted skin,
And the darkest fire burning
Is the soul that lies within.

Lord of his own dance
In the misty morning light,
Surrounded by his clansmen
On that most sacred site.

Whilst naked on the altar
Lies the chosen one,
Whose blood will be the offering,
At the rising of the sun.

Oh, How great would be the honour
To be that sacrificial lamb,
And give yourself so freely
For the benefit of the clan?

And when the darkness closes in,
Their next breath will be their last
As to the sound of beating drums
Their blood runs thick and fast.

To honour Mother Earth
As the sun begins to rise,
The shaman's staff is raised up high,
Amidst the tribal cries.

While the drums beat ever louder,
To the rhythm of the heart.
Then when he taps his staff three times,
The celebrations truly start.

But all that now remains
Of that wondrous divine rite,
Lies beyond the veils of time
Upon that ancient site.

THE BEAT OF MY HEART

Within this sacred circle I stand alone.
A consecrated ritual space,
Where save for the beat of my heart,
I can hear no other sound.

I dedicate this sacred circle to spirits gods and daemons,
From far beyond this realm,
And save for the beat of my heart,
I can hear no other sound.

Yet strong and powerful is the silent voice,
Mysteriously profound,
And save for the beat of my heart,
There is no other sound.

THE FOOL AND THE MAGE

I traverse this universe
Through castles made of sand.
The fool that walks behind the Mage,
And seeks to understand.

Beyond the spheres of linear time
I seek the chequered floor,
While the Mage only sees,
An ever-open door.

And with my eyes tightly shut,
Through that door I can see,
Shamanic witch from ancient times,
And know that she was me.

The primordial chaos in her eyes
Reflects true tranquility,
And all my existential lives
I see with clarity.

And that ethereal gypsy
I followed at the start,
Showed me, that to grow from fool to Mage
I must seek within my heart.

FORGOTTEN CHILDREN

Theres a long, forgotten remnant,
From a time of genocide,
Whose ancestral line,
Is soaked in the blood ...
of a biblical divide.

When so many lives were lost
To that chaotic force,
Save those few who hid,
From the ashen gaze ...
of the rider on pale horse.

And while many, chase the shadows
Of that daemonic line,
Seeking knowledge,
From the sacred fire ...
that burns so deep inside.

Only sons and daughters of the moon,
Children of the morning star
Feel the fire of truth
In every heartbeat ...
and know exactly who they are.

PLANETARY INVOCATION

Dark realms of Saturn wherein are taught
discipline and self-restraint,
I seek to go beyond other's limitations
and push the boundaries of constraint.

And in Jupiter forge my sceptre
of opportunity and transmutation,
and free my soul from the chains
of dogma and religion.

Mars the fire in my blood;
strong, determined and unnerving,
for honesty and truth
are the masters' I am serving.

Venus, be thou ever
the guardian of my soul,
the mistress of love and desire
that makes my spirit whole.

Mercury, I invoke thy caduceus,
twin serpents of regeneration,
breathe new life into my words,
bring the gift of inspiration.

Luna, take me beyond the confines
of the conscious world I see,
into the astral mists where visions
are clear and time flies forever free.

And my shining sun, my Lucifer,
the brightest shining light,
I seek your fire and passion in all I do,
within this, my sacred rite.

FIRE DRAGON

In a solitary cavern,
South of infinity,
Wherein lies the border,
Of myth and certainty.
Sits the watchful guardian,
At the gates of fire,
Whose breath ignites the very spark,
Seeking only to inspire.

While the rhythm of his heart,
Commands the sun to shine,
And with the softest whisper,
True love becomes divine.
Elemental dragon ...
Serpent of desire ...
Who keeps the sacred passion,
Deep within the fire.

LESSON ONE

"Please tell me teacher,
What I should know."
"All in good time, my child,
You will learn,
As you grow,
The wisdom of the wild."

"But I do not Want to wait,
Until I'm old and grey.
What good is it,
To learn so late?
Please teach me it today"

"Such knowledge given
To the young,
Would simply be a waste.
Your first lesson,
Has just begun...
Wisdom cannot be learnt in haste.

And when you too, are old and grey,
And many days have since passed by...
Remember my child,
These words I say,
Time teaches more than I."

LOVE BEYOND RELIGION
(FOR VIX)

Nail my hands upon the tree,
Where once I sat and watched you play,
And know that they still long,
To hold you closer with each day.

Nail my feet as tears I weep,
For sunny days beneath this tree,
Spent watching you from the shade,
Playing wild and free.

Place the crown upon my brow,
Made of thorns that tear my flesh,
And see my blood mixed with tears,
Lamenting all I've lost to death.

Pierce my already broken heart,
So, the love held inside can flow,
Taking me beyond this realm,
To where your light forever glows.

LET THERE BE LIGHT

From the elemental sphere,
an open portal calls to me,
where the shadows,
of my unconscious mind,
seek only to be free.

In an ever-shifting chaos,
where words have no place.
Both infinite,
and non existent,
just pure divine grace.

And with the sword of balance,
forged in the sacrificial fire.
I willingly surrender
all that I am,
and all that I desire.

So, when the veils are lifted,
and the horizon is in sight.
Maybe I will truly,
understand the words,
... Let there be light.

DREAMSTATE

The gates of ancient myth
Stand by an old oak tree,
Where a velvet gothic mist
Lies betwixt the land and sea.

And there I choose to be
Wrapped in shades of darkness,
Where my words have more meaning
When softly whispered in the silence.

For when the world turns upside down
And nothing but chaos seems to rule,
I remember how I walk within
The eternal chaos of the fool.

ANOTHER LIFE

I think I need another life
Or maybe several more,
For the pursuit of wisdom
Is an ever-open door.

And though it is contrariwise
To universal law,
With just a dash of hindsight
I could be so much more.

Id bathe in seas of knowledge,
Then rest upon their shore,
And see all that lies above.
Below... far beyond ... and far before.

POWER OF THE WITCH

Where sorrow punctuates happiness,
And joy mingles softly with despair,
The hope for all the future
Dangles tentatively, upon
The whisper of a prayer.

But still and soft is the beating heart
That cries out in the darkest hour,
For in those silent moments,
Can be felt the eternal strength,
That is the witch's greatest power.

TODAY

If I had the wisdom of tomorrow,
With the hindsight of yesterday,
There'd be nothing left,
For me to learn today.

So, I will wait for tomorrow,
And learn from yesterday,
As I grab with both hands,
The lessons of today.

SOUL SENSES

Can you see the rain
From the rivers point of view?
Or understand the relationship,
Between the meadow and the dew?
And know that the rain cloud,
Is aware from its birth,
The part it will play,
In nourishing the earth?

Can you feel the rhythm of the ocean
As it makes way for the shark?
Or sense how the fire knows,
It was once a spark?
And how each tiny flame,
Knows if it will flicker or blaze,
Since the world was created,
Until the end of days?

How the air that you breathe,
Or the wind on your face,
Has transcended all the mysteries,
Throughout time and space?
Or that each speck of dust
That graces this Earth,
Knew creations intent,
At its primordial birth?

So, when you can feel like the wind,
And commune with the sea,
As you seek to unravel,
The Earths mystery,
And see through the eyes of a fire,
Still feeling the warmth of the sun,
Only then can you know,
Your journeys begun.

SONG OF THE PHOENIX

A burning,
Iridescent blaze,
Of glorious colour
Marks the end of her days.

Imbued with spices,
Of the richest fragrance,
To warm her soul,
And lead the dance.

Of the eternal spirit,
Which never dies,
Despite her heartfelt
And anguished cries.

When at dawns first light,
With her saddest song,
She will lament
For days now gone.

As she gazes once more,
Deep into the eyes,
Of the icy stare
Seeing her own demise.

Until the golden rays,
Of the risen sun
Resurrect her song,
Of new days begun.

THE WITCH

I follow the old path
Of elementals and fey,
Where ancient footsteps
Mark the way.

With one foot in each world
All life I embrace,
Where natural and supernatural
Teach wisdom and grace.

And that which is silent
Whispers quietly to me,
As I search in the dark
For what others can't see.

And as long as the moon
Waxes and wanes,
Vital energy flows freely
Right through my veins.

Father God, and Mother Goddess,
Mystic and Mage,
Enlighten my soul
As I set the stage.

When calm and serene,
In dead of night, black as pitch,
I practice my craft,
For I am a witch.

SWEET UNCERTAINTY

I may never see the sunrise,
Or feel the summer rain,
And it's possible
That I may never,
Grace this Earth again.

And whether I will walk,
Or fly upon the breeze,
Like everything I've yet to know,
Death too remains,
A sweet uncertainty.

I don't know if I'll remember,
Those I loved from yesterday,
Or if, with my last breath,
All memories fade away.
The only thing I know,
With any surety,
Is that whatever,
Happens next,
I will forever be.

www.ingramcontent.com/pod-product-compliance
Lightning Source LLC
Chambersburg PA
CBHW021157080526
44588CB00008B/376